# RAIL FREIGHT IN THE 21ST CENTURY

## PAUL D. SHANNON

AMBERLEY

First published 2022

Amberley Publishing
The Hill, Stroud
Gloucestershire, GL5 4EP

www.amberley-books.com

Copyright © Paul D. Shannon, 2022

The right of Paul D. Shannon to be identified
as the Author of this work has been asserted in
accordance with the Copyrights, Designs and
Patents Act 1988.

ISBN 978 1 3981 1184 4 (print)
ISBN 978 1 3981 1185 1 (ebook)

British Library Cataloguing in Publication Data.
A catalogue record for this book is available from
the British Library.

Origination by Amberley Publishing.
Printed in the UK.

# Introduction

The first two decades of the twenty-first century saw no let-up in the pace of change for the rail freight scene. The Class 66 was still something of a novelty in the early years, while many first-generation diesels remained in service. However, withdrawals took place rapidly as the 66s became established. It was not long before Class 31s and 33s lost their remaining freight work and even the newer Class 56s and 58s were soon superseded. The versatile Class 37s managed to last a little longer in front-line service, while a reduced Class 60 fleet earned its keep on heavy haul duties. Meanwhile, new high-speed Class 67s replaced Class 47s on mail traffic. As for electrics, Class 86s and 90s had plenty of life left in them, but the comparatively new Class 92s struggled to find sustainable work.

Today, a fleet of nearly 500 Class 66s covers most freight duties in Britain, accompanied by smaller numbers of newer types such as Class 68s, 70s and 88s. But some of the older traction has survived against expectations, especially thanks to the smaller freight operators such as Direct Rail Services with its Class 37s and Class 57s, DC Rail with its Class 56s and Class 60s, and Colas Rail with its Class 56s, and GB Railfreight is giving a new lease of life to the Class 56 bodyshell with its Class 69 rebuilds. As for the Class 66s, their monotony is relieved by a large variety of liveries, from the standard colours of the big operators to one-off commemorative and advertising styles.

The competitive market has served rail freight well in the twenty-first century. Back in 2000 there were essentially just three operators: EWS for bulk trainload and wagonload freight, Freightliner for deep-sea containers and Direct Rail Services for nuclear traffic. Freightliner began to stretch its wings with some infrastructure business and then expanded into commercial bulk freight from 2000 onwards. Direct Rail Services also diversified, albeit on a smaller scale. GB Railfreight was an entirely new operator and quickly gained a share of bulk and intermodal flows. Colas Rail entered the freight market with log trains to Chirk and has hauled a number of niche flows, as well as a significant chunk of railway infrastructure traffic. But not all new operators were successful, as shown by the short lives of Advenza and Fastline.

In terms of traffic, the biggest change of the last two decades has been the almost total demise of coal, the former lifeblood of many parts of the rail network. The replacement on a far smaller scale has been biomass. Carryings of steel and petroleum have declined as well, albeit less drastically. Construction traffic such as stone, sand and spoil has grown steadily and brought rail freight back to some previously dormant locations. The logistics market is well served by intermodal trains, carrying both deep-sea and domestic containers on key routes. On the other hand, the wagonload concept has finally been abandoned after its revival by EWS in the late 1990s. Marshalling yards have definitely been confined to the past.

# Aggregates

One of the former National Power locomotives, No. 59204, takes the Westbury route at Fairwood Junction with 7A77, the 11.44 Merehead–Theale train, on 1 February 2018. The six National Power Class 59/2s had joined the EWS fleet in 1998 and EWS was sold to Deutsche Bahn in 2007, which explains the DB Schenker branding illustrated here. All Class 59s used on Mendip operations passed into Freightliner ownership in 2019, heralding yet another change of colour scheme.

The Westbury White Horse overlooks the scene as Aggregates Industries-liveried loco No. 59005 *Kenneth J Painter* approaches Fairwood Junction on 1 February 2018. The train is 6C58, the 11.55 Oxford Banbury Road–Whatley empties. Aggregates Industries had acquired Foster Yeoman and its locomotive fleet in 2006 and the Class 59s were then repainted in blue and turquoise livery.

No. 59001 *Yeoman Endeavour* shunts empty Hanson JHA hoppers at the west end of Acton yard on 28 August 2001. The working is 6V28, the 12.00 from Hither Green to Whatley, which has called at Acton to attach wagons from a discharge terminal in the London area. No. 59001 was one of the original batch of four Class 59s that entered service in February 1986.

The former goods yard at Wool in Dorset was used to load gravel from Warmwell quarry between 2000 and 2014. Initially trains comprised two-axle PGA hoppers and were destined for Neasden. No. 66194 shunts part of its train in Wool station on 17 July 2000 before working 6Z15, the 18.55 departure to Neasden.

Bucking the trend of ever longer and heavier aggregate trains, No. 66011 heads west near Manea with 6M45, the 14.17 Barham–Mountsorrel empties, on 1 July 2014. The two-axle hoppers at the rear of the train were nearing the end of their lives by that time, with replacement bogie vehicles entering service.

One of the most distinctive freight operations in the late twentieth and early twenty-first centuries was the Redland self-discharge train, which used an underfloor conveyor system to discharge wagons without the need for fixed equipment. With the wagons still carrying their original Redland green livery, No. 66083 passes Washwood Heath with 6M31, the 10.42 Banbury–Mountsorrel empties, on 12 August 2015. Unfortunately, an accident with the rotating boom of a self-discharge train at Mountsorrel brought the operation to an abrupt end in 2016.

The Redland self-discharge train made regular visits to Boston Docks when large quantities of stone were needed for constructing wind turbines off the Lincolnshire coast. Former BR shunters Nos D2112 and D3871, then privately preserved but in regular use at Boston, cross the swing bridge connecting the docks with the main line on 7 June 2005. The two locomotives later moved to the Rother Valley Railway and Ecclesbourne Valley Railway respectively.

GBRf loco No. 66711 was repainted in Aggregates Industries livery in 2015 to mark the start of a new five-year contract between the two companies. One of the loading points included in the contract was Coton Hill yard, Shrewsbury. On 26 April 2017, No. 66711 approaches Shrewsbury station with 6M20, the 13.50 Coton Hill–Wellingborough train.

Freightliner gained an increasing share of the limestone traffic from Tunstead quarry, serving a number of destinations in the north-west, East Anglia and the south-east. No. 66615 approaches Bamford with eighteen MWA box wagons forming 6M96, the 14.38 Barrow Hill–Tunstead empties, on 25 June 2018. Barrow Hill was a staging point for some trains routed via the Midland main line.

DB painted five Class 66s in Maritime livery in 2019 to mark the partnership between the two companies for intermodal traffic from Southampton, Felixstowe and London Gateway. However, the locomotives remained part of the common user fleet. On 6 February 2020, No. 66142 *Maritime Intermodal Three* heads south from Crewe with 6V11, the 10.00 Dowlow–Theale limestone train.

No. 66706 *Nene Valley* approaches Great Rocks Junction with 6Z40, the 02.28 Brentford–Tunstead empties, on 16 July 2013. This locomotive was one of the first batch of Class 66s delivered to GB Railfreight and entered service in 2001. The wagons are JGA hoppers originally constructed in 1987 for RH Roadstone and later rebogied for use by Freightliner, followed by transfer to GBRf.

Still carrying its obsolete Loadhaul livery, No. 60059 *Swinden Dalesman* shunts tanks and hoppers beside Dove Holes quarry on 26 May 2009. The tanks carried gas oil to Peak Forest fuelling point at that time. No. 60059 was repainted into DB livery in 2012 and was still on DB's books in early 2022, albeit stored out of use at Toton depot.

Alongside its token passenger service the Guide Bridge–Stockport line provides a useful link between the Peak District quarries and the West Coast main line. No. 66709 *Sorrento* in MSC livery passes Reddish South with 6G92, the 09.44 Peak Forest–Small Heath limestone train, on 26 August 2021. Small Heath was busy at that time feeding HS2 construction sites in the Birmingham area.

The former Kelbit branch at Ashton-in-Makerfield returned to regular use in 2018 to handle limestone from Shap quarry. The loaded trains were split into two portions at Tuebrook sidings because of the short siding length at Ashton-in-Makerfield. GBRf loco No. 60056, still in Colas Railfreight livery but with the word 'Colas' erased, propels its wagons towards the terminal on 15 April 2021 after working 6F64, the 14.10 departure from Tuebrook.

EWS's fleet of two-axle MEA wagons could carry stone as well as coal and found a regular duty from Harrison's sidings, Shap. No. 60096 passes Lowgill just before entering the Lune gorge with 6C40, the 07.20 Carnforth–Harrisons empties, on 6 August 2002. After reloading, the train would return south to Carnforth and then go forward to Ashton-in-Makerfield.

The Settle to Carlisle line received a boost when Arcow quarry gained its new rail connection in 2015. No. 66757 *West Somerset Railway* shunts HYA hoppers at Arcow on 19 October 2016. It had arrived on 6M67, the 22.04 service from Bredbury, and would later form 6M33, the 12.12 departure to Pendleton. The wagons are former coal hoppers, which have been shortened to carry aggregates.

Colas Rail gained a share of the aggregates traffic from South Wales using former Freightliner coal hoppers. No. 70811 passes Alexandra Dock Junction yard, Newport, with 4B45, the 16.30 Pengam–Briton Ferry empties, on 22 August 2017. The train will be loaded with stone at Neath Abbey Wharf. Also visible in the yard are No. 66003 with empty steel carriers for Port Talbot and two further Class 66s with car parts from Bridgend to Dagenham.

# Cement and Blocks

One of the first bulk freight contracts to engage Freightliner instead of EWS covered various cement flows from Hope (Earles Sidings), including a new terminal at Weaste on the Manchester Ship Canal. No. 66503 is pictured at Weaste on 11 August 2000 after working 6J91, the 14.04 departure from Earles Sidings. Unfortunately, this traffic flow did not remain on rail for long.

In the early twenty-first century the sidings at Colnbrook, on the rump of the former Staines West branch, handled incoming cement and fly ash traffic for the building of Heathrow Terminal Five. No. 66529 shunts PCA cement tanks at Colnbrook on 19 August 2003 after arriving with 6V27, the 22.30 departure from Earles Sidings.

EWS gained a new flow of cement from Tunstead to Willesden in 2004 as part of a seven-year contract with Buxton Lime Industries. No.66087 heads north near Leighton Buzzard with bogie JGA tanks forming 6H50, the 12.59 from Willesden to Tunstead, on 12 April 2012. This flow later switched to Freightliner haulage.

Carrying both Bardon Aggregates and Aggregate Industries branding, Freightliner loco No. 66623 *Bill Bolsover* passes Kilby Bridge with 6M92, the 12.42 West Thurrock–Earles Sidings empty cement tanks, on 23 August 2014. The customer branding was removed after Freightliner lost the Bardon contract to GBRf in 2015 and No. 66623 later became the first member of its sub-class to receive Genesee & Wyoming orange livery.

GBRf began moving cement from Padeswood (Penyffordd) to Avonmouth for Hanson in January 2020. Some trains ran via Wolverhampton, while others were routed via the Marches line. No. 66707 *Sir Sam Fay* approaches Craven Arms on 30 May 2021 with thirteen JPA bogie tanks forming 6V41, the 11.20 departure from Penyffordd.

A regular Class 70 duty for Freightliner has been the cement train from Earles Sidings to Walsall, routed via Chesterfield and the freight-only Sheet Stores-Stenson line. No. 70011 is pictured near Sawley with 6G65, the 09.19 departure from Earles Sidings, on 4 November 2021.

For several decades the railway carried Forticrete blocks from Merehead to Acton on the back (or front) of stone trains between those locations. The traffic used modified OAA wagons. Former National Power loco No. 59201 shunts five OAAs after arrival at Acton with 7A09, the 07.12 working from Merehead, on 29 October 2010.

Plasmor began forwarding blocks by rail from its Heck factory in the 1980s and that traffic has continued into the twenty-first century, with up to five trains a week serving Biggleswade and Bow as required. The blocks are carried in two-axle PNA wagons. No. 66128 passes Lincoln Central with 4E25, the 11.29 Bow–Heck empties, on 25 June 2020.

# Infrastructure Traffic

Freightliner won its first contract for transporting railway ballast and other infrastructure materials in 1999, using its existing yard at Crewe Basford Hall as a base. Thirteen Class 66s, Nos 66506–18, were dedicated to this business. On 30 August 2000, No. 66506 shunts the ballast distribution system of the High Output Ballast Cleaner train in Basford Hall up sidings. It has been reloaded with ballast and will now move to Crewe Pre-Assembly Depot for servicing.

Penmaenmawr was a long-standing source of railway ballast and in 2001 a daily train ran from the quarry to Crewe Basford Hall, hauled by Freightliner. No. 66513 draws forward at Penmaenmawr as its last Railtrack-liveried wagon is loaded on 20 August 2001. It will depart as 6K22, the 11.52 service to Basford Hall.

Ballast reaches its destination in two stages: first from the quarry or other loading point to a stockpile or 'virtual quarry', and then from the stockpile to the work site, usually in what are known as possession trains. The possession trains require a different timetable each week depending on the location of the work. One such working, 6W30, the 13.32 from Basford Hall to Bargoed, is pictured at Dorrington on 20 April 2013, topped and tailed by Nos 66113 and 66086.

For many years railway ballast from the remote Glensanda quarry in Scotland has been shipped to Grain for onward movement by train. No. 66740 *Sarah* heads west between Longhedge Junction and Culvert Road Junction with 6E40, the 09.40 Grain–Ferme Park ballast working, on 31 March 2015. The ballast in this instance is destined for the London Underground.

# Coal, Biomass and Nuclear

The merry-go-round system had revolutionised the delivery of coal to power stations in the late 1960s and some rakes of HAA hoppers remained in use in the early 2000s. No. 56018 passes Barnetby with an eastbound train for reloading at Immingham on 16 June 2003.

Opencast coal kept several freight-only lines in south-west Scotland active into the twenty-first century. Loading has already begun at Chalmerston on 28 August 2003, as No. 66216 runs round its train of twenty-nine HAAs. The inward working was 6R72, the 14.35 departure from Falkland yard.

Providing non-standard traction for an empty merry-go-round train is No. 37886, pictured just after passing under Warrington Bank Quay station on 4 September 2000. The working is 6P57, the 11.30 from Fiddlers Ferry to Warrington Arpley, and the wagons are a mixture of standard HAAs and the hooded HFA variant.

After National Power gave up the haulage of Drax coal trains, its JMA hopper wagons passed to EWS and were redeployed on Fiddlers Ferry workings. Still looking smart in its obsolete Mainline Freight livery, No. 60078 approaches Monks Siding on the outskirts of Warrington with 7F81, the 07.43 departure from Liverpool Bulk Terminal, on 1 August 2001.

Freightliner supplied Fiddlers Ferry with trainloads of imported coal from Manisty Wharf, Ellesmere Port. No. 66608 crawls through the Fiddlers Ferry hopper house at 0.5 mph on 25 October 2006 after working 6F02, the 12.13 departure from Ellesmere Port. This flow ceased in 2015 and Fiddlers Ferry received its last coal train in 2019.

Hatfield colliery was closed by British Coal in 1993 but was revived three times in the years that followed. It finally wound its last coal in June 2015, by which time only two other deep mines in the UK – Kellingley and Thoresby – remained in production. No. 66562 departs from Hatfield with 6M75, the 11.39 to Ratcliffe, on 31 March 2008.

Open access operator Fastline won a five-year contract to transport coal for E.ON starting in April 2008 and acquired a fleet of five Class 66s and ninety-four IIA hopper wagons for the business. Unfortunately, the contract was cut short in March 2010 when Fastline's parent company Jarvis went into administration. No. 66305 heads south at Hasland with 6G71, the 12.29 from Hatfield to Ratcliffe, on 25 June 2009.

Drax was the last coal-fired power station to be built in Britain and by far the biggest, with a generating capacity of 4,000 megawatts. It gradually switched from taking home-produced to imported coal as the local pits closed. No. 66712 *Peterborough Power Signalbox* is pictured at Drax with 6H93, the 07.35 service from Tyne Dock, on 30 March 2010.

Avonmouth supplied trainloads of imported coal to Didcot from 1993 until 2013. The increase in 60-mph freight trains sharing tracks with InterCity 125s justified the building of long passing loops between Wantage Road and Challow. However, in this instance No. 66186 is staying on the Up fast line as it passes Denchworth with 6D11, the 08.27 from Avonmouth to Didcot, on 30 October 2012.

The reopening of Boldon East Curve made it easier for coal trains from Tyne Dock to use the coastal route via Sunderland and Eaglescliffe instead of the busier East Coast main line via Durham. No. 66729 *Derby County* passes Eaglescliffe with 6H93, the 08.43 Tyne–Drax working, on 16 August 2013. Some of the hopper wagons retain the markings of their former operator, Fastline.

In 2011, Colas Rail Freight won a contract to move opencast coal from Wolsingham on the Weardale line to Ratcliffe and Scunthorpe, using Freightliner HHA hopper wagons. No. 66849 *Wylam Dilly* passes Crowle with 6Z42, the 10.30 Wolsingham–Scunthorpe service, on 22 August 2011. This locomotive was formerly Freightliner No. 66576.

The Settle to Carlisle line was upgraded to carry heavy coal trains from Scottish ports and opencast sites to English power stations, although this traffic turned out to be shorter-lived than expected. No. 66523 crosses Arten Gill viaduct near Dent with 6M11, the 05.49 Hunterston–Fiddlers Ferry train, on 18 April 2014.

Several deep mines in Nottinghamshire survived into the twenty-first century. The last to close was Thoresby, which brought its final coal to the surface in July 2015. No. 66510 has just run round its train at Thoresby Colliery Junction while working 6B58, the 08.30 from Thoresby to West Burton, on 17 February 2015.

The cooling towers and chimneys of Ferrybridge power station rise over the lineside trees as No. 66764 approaches Whitley Bridge station with 6H12, the 06.25 Tyne Dock–Drax coal train, on 7 April 2015. At that time the haulage of Drax coal trains was shared between DB Schenker (formerly EWS), Freightliner and GB Railfreight.

GB Railfreight loco No. 66789 in retro BR livery hauls former DB HTA hopper wagons towards Middlesbrough on 4 December 2019. The working is 4N05, the 08.40 Doncaster–Redcar empties, which after loading with imported coal will return south as 6M06 to Doncaster. The haulage of HTA hoppers requires buckeye couplings and the only members of the GBRf fleet to have this feature are Nos 66780–89.

In South Wales, the last deep mine closed in 2008 but opencast coal was still being transported from two sites – Cwmbargoed and Onllwyn – in 2020. No. 66100 arrives at Onllwyn with empty HTA hoppers forming 4O32, the 08.47 departure from Margam, on 21 July 2020. After loading the train would form an overnight service to Immingham.

In the late 1980s Cawoods acquired a fleet of two-axle low-floor flat wagons, coded PFA, to carry its 20-foot containers with coal for export to Ireland. After that traffic finished, the resources were used on other flows and some of the containers were rebranded British Fuels. No. 56089 leaves Healey Mills yard with 6Z51, the 12.30 special to Immingham, on 25 August 2000.

The Class 58s spent much of their short lives hauling merry-go-round trains in and around the East Midlands, but in later years the class strayed further afield. No. 58033 passes Hinksey, Oxford, with a rake of MEA wagons forming 6M14, the 14.25 from Avonmouth to Rugby, on 23 July 2001. The load was imported coal for Rugby Cement.

The rail terminal at Tyne Dock switched from exporting North East coal to importing foreign coal and later to importing biomass, destined for Drax and Lynemouth. GB Railfreight became the dominant operator at the port. No. 66733 is about to haul its train under the biomass silo at Tyne after working 4N99, the 11.00 departure from Drax, on 11 July 2011.

Ironbridge power station took biomass by rail from 2013 until the facility closed completely in 2015. Alongside deliveries in hopper wagons, some of the biomass was conveyed in containers from Seaforth intermodal terminal. No. 66707 *Sir Sam Fay* heads south from Crewe with 4G01, the 05.34 Seaforth–Ironbridge train, on 27 August 2014.

Immingham became one of the entry ports for biomass to Drax. A loading facility was built alongside the Killingholme branch at the north end of the port. No. 66152 has just run round its loaded IIA hoppers at the start of its journey with 6H77, the 16.15 from Immingham to Drax, on 28 September 2017.

Biomass traffic to Lynemouth kept much of the Blyth & Tyne network alive pending its planned conversion to a passenger route. No. 66757 passes Marcheys House, just south of Ashington, with 6N87, the 13.32 Lynemouth–Tyne Dock empties, on 3 January 2020. The Class 66s on this route later gave way to Class 60s.

GBRf biomass trains from Liverpool to Drax normally run via Warrington and Northwich to avoid Miles Platting bank on the more direct route. Former Colas loco No. 60096 approaches Moore with 6E10, the 11.15 departure from Liverpool Biomass Terminal, on 25 September 2020. The Drax-branded IIA wagons were first introduced in 2014.

A short section of single track at Strand Road was doubled in 2021 to enable parallel movements into and out of Liverpool Docks. On 7 September 2021, No. 60087 accelerates over the new trackwork before tackling the gradient to Bootle with 6E10, the 11.15 service to Drax. No. 60087 was one of the ten Class 60s that GBRf acquired from Colas in 2018 and one of the first to carry GBRf colours.

During the period when nuclear flask trains no longer had a brake van but still required barrier wagons, Nos 20315 and 20308 pass Stableford with 7M56, the 13.27 from Berkeley to Crewe, on 22 June 2001. No. 20315 was withdrawn and scrapped in 2013, while No. 20308 was still on DRS's books in 2021, albeit out of use.

Sizewell 'A' power station stopped generating electricity in 2006, but the defuelling process kept regular flask trains from the railhead at Leiston running until 2014. Nos 37402 and 37603 have just passed the gated level crossing at Knodishall with 6M69, the 15.42 from Leiston to Crewe, on 21 February 2014.

Pairings of Class 37s and 57s were never particularly common, but on 9 May 2014 Nos 37601 and 57010 are pictured at Rowton hauling 6K41, the 14.58 Valley–Crewe flask train. No. 37601 was one of the Class 37s converted for European passenger services but sold to DRS when plans for locomotive-hauled passenger trains via the Channel Tunnel were abandoned. Regular flask movements from Valley ceased in 2019.

# Minerals and Waste

Freight trains returned to the former Great Central main line north of Loughborough when EWS started carrying containerised desulphogypsum to Hotchley Hill in 1998. A short loading pad was built just north of the platforms of Rushcliffe halt. No. 66219 draws forward ready for the next few containers to be exchanged on 26 July 2001. It will later depart as 6E76, the 12.03 to Milford sidings.

It was desulphogypsum from Drax power station that brought freight back to the Settle to Carlisle line in 1993. GBRf shared the business with EWS from 2002 onwards. No. 66719 *Metro-Land* passes Settle Junction with 4M91, the 13.16 from West Burton to Kirkby Thore, on 9 April 2008. The Metronet livery related to a contract to deliver infrastructure materials to the London Underground.

As the supply of desulphogypsum from power stations declined, the plasterboard factory at Kirkby Thore began to take trainloads of imported gypsum from Hull Docks. No. 66021 heads south from Ribblehead with 6E95, the 10.44 Kirkby Thore–Hull empty box wagons, on 19 October 2016.

GBRf took over haulage of industrial sand trains from Middleton Towers to Barnby Dun, Monk Bretton and Goole in 2013. No. 66716 pauses alongside the former Royal Mail terminal at Doncaster Down Decoy yard with 6E88, the 12.39 from Middleton Towers to Goole, on 4 August 2014. The two-axle PAA wagons were later replaced by bogie IIA vehicles.

The former Ravenhead oil sidings at St Helens returned to use for glassworks sand from Middleton Towers in 2016. DB stopped handling this traffic in early 2020, but it later resumed with DC Rail haulage. No. 60046 *William Wilberforce* passes Whittlesea with eighteen JNA wagons forming 6Z18, the 08.33 from Middleton Towers to Ravenhead, on 17 July 2021.

Because of the poor availability of its own small fleet of Class 60s, DC Rail hired traction from other companies on several occasions. One instance was the use of Colas Rail No. 56049 on 7 June 2021. It is pictured passing St Helens Central with 4Z14, the 09.00 empties from Ravenhead to Chaddesden.

Cornish china clay operations survived into the twenty-first century, but on a much reduced scale compared with the 1990s. One locomotive operated the Fowey trains to and from Goonbarrow and the Parkandillack branch as required, while a second locomotive covered the weekly circuit between Cornwall and the Potteries. No. 66147 shunts CDAs at Kernick on the Parkandillack branch on 12 April 2011, having worked the 6P07 empties from Fowey.

Long-distance Cornish china clay traffic still used several different wagon types and served several different destinations at the beginning of the century. No. 60032 *William Booth* passes Washwood Heath with 6V70, the 08.57 Cliffe Vale–St Blazey empties, on 23 February 2001. The slurry tanks at the front of the train had originated in Scotland and joined this train at Bescot.

Freightliner held the contract to move potash, polyhalite and salt from Boulby to Tees Dock and Middlesbrough from 2007 until 2021. No. 66532 heads inland at Hunt Cliff on the Boulby branch with twelve JIA hoppers forming 6F24, the 12.28 from Boulby to Tees Dock, on 22 April 2021.

When still in full production the iron- and steel-making complex on Teesside required deliveries of both limestone and lime. The two flows often travelled in the same train as far as Tees yard before splitting into separate trip workings. On 1 June 2007, No. 60045 *The Permanent Way Institution* passes Grangetown with the 6N25 trip from Tees yard to Redcar, comprising limestone hoppers from Shap.

Possibly the longest-standing block mineral train in Britain is the limestone flow from Tunstead to Brunner Mond at Northwich. In 2020 this train ran usually four times a week and was a reliable target for Class 60 haulage. No. 60044 *Dowlow* passes one of the few remaining semaphores on the Mid-Cheshire line at Plumley West hauling 6H02, the 09.30 Warrington Arpley–Tunstead empties, on 20 October 2020.

The Roxby branch north of Scunthorpe has been busy for several decades with various flows of waste and spoil to fill the extensive ironstone pits in the area. No. 66101 arrives at Roxby with SSA wagons after working 6E58, the 22.44 departure from Angerstein Wharf, on 10 September 2020. The MBA wagons on the second track are waiting to return to Rossington.

Household waste trains from Greater Manchester were diverted to the energy from waste plant at Runcorn from 2013 onwards, providing long-term traffic for the Folly Lane branch. No. 70010 has just uncoupled from its train at Folly Lane on 19 April 2021 after working 6F33, the 09.16 service from Bredbury.

# Metals

Several years after EWS took over the bulk rail freight business, Nos 56090 and 56074 provide a reminder of the brief Loadhaul era of the 1990s as they approach Hatfield & Stainforth station on 14 August 2001. The train is 6D51, the 08.01 Enterprise feeder service from Doncaster to Hull, conveying four BEAs with steel for export.

The flow of imported zinc from Grimsby to Bloxwich was revived thanks to the EWS Enterprise network, joining other traffic on the trunk haul from Immingham to Bescot. No. 56069 crawls into Immingham sorting sidings on 7 August 2002 with 6G44, the 15.08 trip from Grimsby, comprising a mixture of VGA, VAA and VKA vans.

Associated British Ports and British Steel provided a new steel terminal in Newport Docks in 1997, catering for the growing export traffic at that time. No. 09105 shunts a mixed rake of covered steel carriers at the terminal on 26 October 2000. The locomotive was formerly No. 08835 and was regeared for higher speed running to become a Class 09 in 1993.

Rail-making continued at Workington steelworks until 2006, when production moved to an upgraded facility at Scunthorpe. Main-line traffic at Workington consisted of inward steel blooms from Teesside and outward rail to various destinations in Britain and overseas. Hunslet 0-4-0 diesel-hydraulic shunter No. 404 shunts a rake of Cargowaggon rail carriers at Workington on 30 August 2002.

After the coil plate mill at Teesside closed in 2001, Corby tube works received its coil feedstock from South Wales instead. No. 60066 *John Logie Baird* passes Washwood Heath with 15 BZA coil carriers forming 6Z42, the 02.11 from Margam to Corby, on 23 February 2001. The BZA wagons were converted from BAAs by the addition of cradles.

The railway carried intermittent flows of steel to Purfleet for export to mainland Europe, sometimes in block trains and sometimes in wagonload consignments. No. 66090 passes Purfleet station with 6L68, the 21.22 Cardiff Tidal–Purfleet train, on 24 August 2001, comprising BDA and BRA steel carriers.

The Immingham-Santon (Scunthorpe) iron ore flow was the first of its kind to use rotary-coupled tippler wagons in the early 1970s. It also became the last such flow following the closure of other steel-making plants. No. 60097 *Port of Grimsby & Immingham* is an appropriate choice of motive power for 6K22, the 09.42 empties from Santon, as it arrives at Immingham on 7 August 2002.

EWS introduced a fleet of sliding hood coil carriers in the late 1990s, often nicknamed 'pig pens' because of their shape. They were used alongside other types to carry moisture-sensitive cold reduced coil. No. 60078 waits for the road at Doncaster on 13 April 2004 with 6D66, the 15.03 Immingham–Doncaster Belmont train, comprising a mixture of BYA, BWA and BIA wagons.

Semaphore signals remained in use at East Usk Junction long after the main line was resignalled. This bracket signal controlled the connection from the Uskmouth branch. No. 66204 passes by on the Down relief line with 6B04, the 15.40 Llanwern–Margam empty steel carriers, on 19 August 2009.

The Up yard at Hitchin saw brief use as a scrap metal terminal, with material brought to the site by road. No. 66021 is about to pull out onto the main line north of Hitchin station with JNA wagons forming 6Z66, the 16.50 departure to Sheerness, on 28 August 2008. The scrap traffic later ceased, but the yard has remained in use to receive aggregates.

In March 2009 Colas Rail took over the regular weekly flow of steel coil for Toyota from Belgium to Burton-on-Trent, making it the first operator other than EWS/DB to haul Channel Tunnel rail freight. No. 47727 is pictured at Burton-on-Trent on 9 April 2009, ready to depart with 6Z48, the 13.05 empties to Dollands Moor.

EWS gained a flow of aluminium ingots from Anglesey Aluminium to Braunau am Inn in Austria in 2005. A weekly feeder service ran between the Anglesey plant and Warrington Arpley yard, where it connected with the Enterprise network. No. 66148 sets back into the plant on 22 August 2009 after working 6D19, the 06.40 empty vans from Arpley.

In 2010, Direct Rail Services made a brief foray into scrap metal movements from Tyne Dock and Stockton to Sheerness. Nos 37682 and 37688 head south at Harrowden on the Midland main line with 6Z92, the 09.20 Stockton-Sheerness scrap train, on 27 August 2010. Sheerness steelworks closed in 2012.

Rows of mainly stored wagons occupy many of the sidings at Tees yard as No. 66034 sets out with 6V02, the 18.43 departure to Margam, on 11 July 2011. The containers are loaded with lime from Thrislington to Port Talbot steelworks, while the coil wagons are returning empty from Hartlepool to South Wales.

Colas Rail started moving coil from Llanwern to Tilbury for export in December 2013 and this later developed into a regular combined train from Margam and Llanwern. The wagons included DB-owned BYA wagons as well as Captrain and GERS hooded flats. No. 60076 passes Pilning with 6V62, the 10.44 Tilbury-Llanwern empties, on 15 April 2015.

A.V. Dawson developed its Middlesbrough rail terminal in the twenty-first century for flows of steel coil, rock salt and tar. The coil arrived on an overnight train from South Wales, with the wagons returning empty later in the day to Tees yard. On 4 December 2019, No. 66077 *Benjamin Gimbert GC* has just set out from the Middlesbrough terminal with 6N27, the 12.15 trip to Tees.

Despite the savage cutbacks in the steel industry on Teesside, the special sections mill at Skinningrove continued to generate rail freight, with semi-finished steel arriving from Scunthorpe via Tees yard when required. No. 66206 passes the long abandoned fan house for Skelton iron mine as it nears its destination with 6N40, the 13.40 trip from Tees yard, on 22 April 2021.

Although EWS and its successor DB have tended to dominate the market for steel traffic between South Wales, Scunthorpe and the North East, GB Railfreight traction made an appearance in 2021. No. 66739 *Bluebell Railway* passes Alexandra Dock Junction yard, Newport, with 6V31, the 00.55 Scunthorpe–Margam slab train, on 16 June 2021.

Over the years the Celsa plant at Cardiff has sent wire rod in coil and other finished products to various destinations by rail. The main flow in 2021 was a weekly train to Burton-on-Trent, using VGA and VKA vans. No. 66117 passes Ley, between Lydney and Gloucester, with 6M37, the 10.03 Cardiff Tidal–Burton train, on 15 June 2021.

Although the days of integrated steel-making at Shotton are a distant memory, the plant has continued to receive trainloads of coil from South Wales for coating. No. 60001 has just crossed the Dee estuary at Hawarden Bridge with 6V75, the 09.24 Dee Marsh Junction–Margam empties, on 13 August 2021.

# Petroleum and Chemicals

Grangemouth refinery is the last source of petroleum traffic in Scotland. In recent years its main flow has been to Dalston in Cumbria, while less frequent trains have run to Prestwick and Sinfin (Derby). On 27 August 2003 No. 66239 nears its journey's end with 6S36, the 08.25 Dalston–Grangemouth empty tank train. Colas Rail took over this flow in 2015.

Freightliner gained a share of the petroleum traffic from Lindsey and Humber refineries in 2001, using two Class 66 locomotives from its recently formed heavy haul fleet. No. 66615 enters the loop at Elford with twenty-six TEA tanks forming 6M00, the 11.23 Humber–Kingsbury service, on 23 July 2004. All Lindsey and Humber traffic reverted to EWS haulage in the following year.

Colas Rail hauled aviation fuel from Lindsey refinery to Colnbrook for Heathrow Airport between 2015 and 2018. No. 60096 passes East Hyde on the Hertfordshire/Bedfordshire border with 6E38, the 13.54 Colnbrook–Lindsey empties, on 19 March 2018. Colas Rail sold all ten of its Class 60s to GB Railfreight later that year.

Heathrow Airport switched its source of supply to Grain in 2018 and the haulage contract went to Freightliner, who introduced a fleet of forty-two bogie tank wagons. No. 66606 is stabled at Colnbrook on 1 April 2019 after arriving with 6V04, the 08.05 service from Grain. Deliveries of fuel to Colnbrook stopped altogether during the 2020/21 pandemic and later restarted at a reduced frequency, with GBRf taking over the haulage.

After the closure of Robeston refinery near Milford Haven in 2015, Puma Energy acquired the site as a storage and distribution terminal and rail traffic continued much as before. No. 60063 passes Bishton gate box near Llanwern with 6B13, the 05.00 Robeston–Westerleigh tank train, on 16 March 2020.

Bitumen was delivered from Lindsey refinery to Ashton-in-Makerfield until 2004, when the flow was diverted to the reopened terminal at Preston Dock. No. 56090 propels its discharged tanks onto the main line at Ashton-in-Makerfield on 9 April 2003, ready to return across the Pennines. The propelling movement was necessary because the terminal had no run-round facility.

A few railway fuelling points still received gas oil by rail in the early 2000s, including several on the former Western Region, which were supplied from Fawley. No. 66213 shunts gas oil tanks at Burngullow on 31 March 2008, before departing as 6C21, the 13.30 trip to Long Rock depot. This flow switched to road haulage in 2013.

The last traffic flow on the freight-only Ravenhead branch from St Helens was sulphuric acid from Hays Chemicals, destined for Roche Pharmaceuticals at Dalry. In later years a trip working from Ravenhead fed into the EWS Enterprise network at Warrington. No. 56119 sets out from the Hays plant with 6F88, the 12.00 trip to Warrington, on 11 August 2000. The traffic ceased when the plant closed in 2002.

The Albion Chemicals plant at Sandbach was a long-standing user of rail freight, sending out various chemicals by rail including liquid chlorine, caustic soda and nitric acid. However, the last traffic to be loaded in these sidings was hydrochloric acid, delivered by road from Runcorn and destined for Dalry. That traffic finished in January 2007. Former BR loco No. 08523 shunts six purged hydrochloric acid tanks on 14 February 2007 in readiness for their removal for storage at Shirebrook.

# Automotive

Bordesley sidings were used as a loading terminal for Land Rover vehicles manufactured at Solihull. Pilot loco No. 08543 in Railfreight grey livery shunts a rake of French-registered IFA car carriers at Bordesley on 23 February 2001. These wagons would be tripped to Washwood Heath and then join a trunk service to Italy via the Channel Tunnel.

Freightliner held a share of the automotive market from 1999 until 2005, hauling trains from Dagenham, Southampton and Portbury to Garston and Mossend. On 15 July 2002, No. 47150 passes South Kenton with 6M26, the 14.05 from Dagenham to Crewe Basford Hall, conveying Ford Focus cars.

The former Baddesley colliery branch was relaid in 2002 to serve the TNT Logistics/Volkswagen parts distribution centre at Birch Coppice. No. 37042 prepares to depart from Birch Coppice exchange sidings with the daily trip working to Bescot on 23 October 2002, conveying empty vans for return to Germany. This traffic ceased with the general rundown of Channel Tunnel freight, but Birch Coppice container terminal was later built on an adjacent site and has remained busy into the 2020s.

Colas Rail temporarily took over haulage of the British leg of the Valencia–Dagenham car parts train in 2009. On hire from Hanson Traction, No. 56311 snakes through Ripple Lane yard with 7Z98, the 05.20 Dollands Moor–Dagenham working, on 27 August 2009. This locomotive would later be rebuilt and re-engined as No. 69002 for GB Railfreight.

The long-established flow of Ford cars between Dagenham and Garston has been mainly diesel-hauled in recent decades, but DB used a Class 92 electric for a time. No. 92031 heads south near Hartford with 6L48, the 16.31 Garston–Dagenham empties, on 16 August 2012. This flow switched to Direct Rail Services haulage in January 2020.

A wide variety of wagon types has appeared on automotive trains in the twenty-first century. Passing Cholsey on 19 August 2013 is No. 66221 with 6X44, the 14.38 Dagenham–Didcot train, conveying Ford vans and cars for Mossend. The consist includes examples of the four-unit two-axle IPA (4384 series) with stanchions, the two-unit two-axle IPA (4333 series), the four-unit two-axle IFA (4376 series) and, at the rear, the double-deck four-unit two-axle IPA (4375 series).

In expectation of a Channel Tunnel bonanza, BR acquired a large fleet of five-unit fully enclosed car carriers, coded WIA. In practice these wagons saw only limited use on Channel Tunnel traffic, but they appeared on various domestic flows, especially from Cowley, Castle Bromwich and Halewood. On 22 August 2014, No. 66128 approaches Eastleigh with 4M52, the 11.32 from Southampton Eastern Docks to Castle Bromwich.

Colas Rail took over the haulage of Ford engines from Bridgend to Dagenham from October 2017 until June 2019, when Ford announced the closure of its Bridgend plant. No. 56105 passes West Ealing with 6L39, the 05.00 Bridgend–Dagenham train, on 1 April 2019. The IVA vans went into storage after this flow finished, with no further revenue-earning use expected.

# Intermodal

Felixstowe has retained its position as Britain's busiest container port and rail traffic has continued to grow. No. 66730 waits to depart from Felixstowe North terminal on 7 April 2010 with 4M23, the 10.59 service to Hams Hall. The First logo is a reminder that GBRf's parent company GB Railways was owned by First Group from 2003 until 2010.

No. 66537 just north of Peterborough with 4E55, the 15.20 Felixstowe–Doncaster intermodal train, on 16 June 2011. The Down Stamford line between Peterborough and Helpston doubles up as a Down slow line for the East Coast route, which explains the partial electrification at this point.

The cross-country route via Ely and Stowmarket has come under increasing pressure due to the growth in Felixstowe traffic, especially as paths are scarce on the alternative route via London. On 29 March 2014, No. 66717 *Good Old Boy* has just come off the single-track section at Soham with 4L20, the 12.44 from Hams Hall to Parkeston yard. The train will be worked forward later from Parkeston to Felixstowe.

No. 66414 was one of the ten Direct Rail Services Class 66s sold to Freightliner in 2011 and later became one of the first members of the class to carry Freightliner's Powerhaul livery. It is pictured leaving Ely with 4L85, the 11.18 Tinsley–Felixstowe North intermodal, on 16 July 2021.

Class 90s replaced the last of Freightliner's Class 86 diagrams in early 2021. Passing Cattawade near Manningtree on 7 February 2022 are Nos 90045 and 90008 with 4L91, the 09.04 Wembley–Felixstowe North train. No. 90008 was one of the thirteen locomotives acquired from Greater Anglia in 2020 after hauled passenger trains gave way to units on the Great Eastern main line.

Channel Tunnel rail freight was one of the greatest disappointments of the early twenty-first century, but in the early years the railway did reasonably well with intermodal traffic between Britain and northern Italy. Pictured at Dollands Moor on 31 May 2001 is No. 92038 *Voltaire* with train 4M76 to Trafford Park, conveying swapbodies and containers from Bari.

The buildings of the former Ripple Lane diesel depot are visible in the background as No. 66042 threads its way through the yard with 6M65, the 14.05 feeder service from Purfleet to Wembley, on 24 August 2001. The bulk containers are destined for Barry and Seaforth and are carried on a mixture of FKA, FIA and FCA wagons.

Freight paths through Stratford are limited by the frequent passenger service out of London Liverpool Street, but electrically hauled trains to and from East Anglia must go this way. Nos 86614 and 86637 pass Stratford with 4L97, the 04.56 Trafford Park–Ipswich train, on 3 April 2002.

Tilbury Riverside freight terminal was established on the site of the passenger terminus that closed in 1992. It handled a mixture of intermodal and conventional wagonload traffic. Pictured shunting at Riverside on 22 October 2002 is No. 57006 *Freightliner Reliance*, having arrived with the 4R90 service from Felixstowe.

With Westfield shopping centre visible on the right, No. 66597 passes Carpenters Road North Junction on the approach to Stratford with 4L89, the 04.10 Crewe Basford Hall–Felixstowe train, on 20 August 2014. The track curving to the left gives access to Bow Goods, while the two tracks behind the locomotive are used by the North London line passenger service.

GB Railfreight attempted a new intermodal flow via the Channel Tunnel in February 2018, carrying Peroni beer from Padova in northern Italy to Tilbury. The plan was for a single set of wagons to complete the out and back trip each week. No. 66775 *HMS Argyll* approaches Dagenham Dock with the last stage of the journey, 4L19, the 09.17 Wembley–Tilbury, on 24 February 2018. Unfortunately the service did not perform well and was withdrawn in May.

Direct Rail Services introduced two daily services on the relatively short route between Daventry International Freight Terminal and the Thames estuary. Initially one train served Ripple Lane and Purfleet, and the other Tilbury. No. 66431 passes Cow Roast near Tring with 4L48, the 13.09 from Daventry to Purfleet, on 25 February 2018. This train was later replaced by a second service to Tilbury.

*Above*: The first of Freightliner's twelve Class 57 locomotives entered service in 1998. They were a useful stopgap before the introduction of the Class 66s. No. 57005 *Freightliner Excellence* is pictured at Southampton Maritime after arrival with train 4O27 from Crewe on 6 September 2000. Freightliner transferred its Class 57s to other operators from 2007 onwards.

*Right*: Freightliner deployed some of its Class 70s on Southampton traffic in order to handle longer, heavier trains. No. 70009 shunts a pair of 60-foot container flats in the additional sidings at Southampton Maritime on 22 August 2014, having arrived on 4O54, the 06.12 departure from Leeds.

In 2001 Freightliner responded to a motive power shortage by hiring some redundant Class 37s from European passenger services. Still showing its extra jumper cables for passenger stock and cast Channel Tunnel roundels, No. 37602 approaches Didcot with 4O24, the 09.34 from Crewe to Southampton, on 23 July 2001.

One disadvantage with fixed length trains is that they sometimes carry a lot of 'fresh air'. A case in point is this working of 4O09, the 10.18 from Trafford Park to Southampton, seen passing Hinksey on the south side of Oxford on 17 July 2013.

The Freightliner mini-terminal at Bristol reopened in 2010, initially to handle trainloads of imported wine from Tilbury, Thamesport and Felixstowe. No. 66534 *OOCL Express* pulls away from the terminal with 4L32, the 11.00 departure to Tilbury, on 27 July 2011. Most of the traffic handled here was transferred to Wentloog in July 2019, but the site remained in railway use as an aggregates loading point.

By 2019 the pattern of trains serving Bristol West had changed, with scheduled trains running to Felixstowe, London Gateway and Southampton. No. 66548 passes North Somerset Junction on the approach to Bristol with 4V31, the 07.53 service from London Gateway, on 5 March 2019.

Direct Rail Services launched its Daventry to Wentloog train in 2012, carrying Tesco 'Less CO2' boxes for the Welsh market. The low height of the boxes meant that when necessary the train could be diverted via routes with a restricted loading gauge. No. 66301 *Kingmoor TMD* passes Badgeworth with 4V44, the 10.47 from Daventry to Wentloog, on 15 February 2018.

Intermodal traffic from Barry Docks was one of the last flows carried by DB's dying wagonload network. After October 2017 Freightliner was able to accommodate the traffic by running a feeder service between Barry and Wentloog. On 20 July 2020, No. 66526 approaches its destination at Barry Docks with 4B48, the 09.36 departure from Wentloog.

GB Railfreight adopted Hams Hall as its main site for intermodal traffic in the West Midlands. No. 66710 shunts wagons at the terminal on 23 October 2002 after arriving from Felixstowe. The wagons on the left are loaded with swapbodies from northern Italy, which was still a significant flow at that time. By early 2022 GBRf was running three trains a day from Felixstowe to Hams Hall, plus a daily service from London Gateway.

Birmingham Lawley Street opened in 1969, supplementing Dudley as the second Freightliner terminal in the West Midlands. It was still busy in the early twenty-first century, with trains to and from the major container ports. On the dank afternoon of 31 October 2003, Lawley Street is host to No. 57003 as it shunts a mixed rake of intermodal stock, including two Tiphook KTA pocket wagons.

Fastline launched its first intermodal service in 2006, linking Thamesport with Doncaster Railport. It later introduced services to Birch Coppice and Trafford Park. The company acquired a fleet of FEA wagons and a trio of ex-BR Class 56 locomotives. Unfortunately, the loadings were inconsistent and Fastline withdrew from the intermodal market in March 2009. No. 56302 passes Ryecroft Junction with 4O90, the 13.36 from Birch Coppice to Thamesport, on 14 February 2007.

DB's predecessor EWS gained a foothold in the intermodal market using its Enterprise wagonload network, but this gradually shifted to trainload operation to and from the deep-sea ports in direct competition with Freightliner and GBRf. No. 66097 passes the north end of the Hatton triangle with 4M66, the 09.32 from Southampton Western Docks to Birch Coppice, on 11 May 2012.

Still in DRS livery but then recently transferred to the Freightliner fleet, No. 66418 passes Sutton Bridge Junction, Shrewsbury, with 4V64, the 11.08 Crewe Basford Hall–Wentloog train, on 22 September 2012. Visible behind the locomotive are Network Rail's Coleham sidings and depot.

The Coventry–Leamington Spa line was singled in the early 1970s at a time when it carried only limited freight traffic. However, the line reopened as a passenger route in 1977 and it has also seen increased usage by Southampton intermodal trains, stretching its capacity at certain times of day. Heading south at Old Milverton on 29 October 2018 is No. 66085 with 4O21, the 09.12 Trafford Park–Southampton intermodal.

DB-liveried locos Nos 90040 and 90018 are about to be overtaken by a London-bound Pendolino as they pass Cathiron, between Nuneaton and Rugby, with 4M25, the 06.06 Mossend–Daventry intermodal, on 23 May 2019. At that time this was the only DB freight working on the West Coast main line to be rostered for electric haulage.

In recent years Direct Rail Services has put its Class 88 electro-diesels to good use on intermodal trains between North Thamesside, Daventry and central Scotland. No. 88008 *Ariadne* nears its destination with 4M27, the 05.46 Mossend–Daventry working, on 19 September 2019. The wagons are mostly IDA low-platform flats, each carrying a single 40-foot or 45-foot container.

Regular trains to the new East Midlands Gateway terminal began in early 2020 and by the end of the year DB, Freightliner and GBRf were all serving the facility. No. 66006 negotiates the new trackwork as it approaches the terminal with 4M79, the 08.00 intermodal from Felixstowe South, on 29 May 2020.

It was the Mediterranean Shipping Company (MSC) that kick-started GBRf's incursion into the intermodal market in 2002. At least half a dozen MSC boxes are included in this working of 4L04, the 14.36 from Hams Hall to Felixstowe South, as it passes Langham Junction behind No. 66765 on 31 July 2020. The massively over-engineered signal post contrasts oddly with the traditional semaphore arms.

With less than a year to go before their retirement, Nos 86622 and 86613 pass Chorlton, south of Crewe, with 4M87, the 11.13 Felixstowe–Trafford Park train, on 24 June 2020. No. 86622 was one of two members of the class to have received Powerhaul livery. Both locomotives had entered service in 1965, numbered E3174 and E3128 respectively.

With long-withdrawn locos Nos 86251 and 90050 languishing in the Down side siding and other, more recently retired, Class 86s visible on the left, No 70015 slows down for its booked stop on the independent lines at Crewe Basford Hall on 19 May 2021. The train is 4M61, the 12.56 from Southampton Maritime to Trafford Park.

In summer 2020 Direct Rail Services was running three daily intermodal trains between Mossend and Daventry, making this the busiest corridor for non-maritime container traffic in Britain. No. 88006 *Juno* heads south at Daresbury with 4M27, the 05.48 Mossend–Daventry service, on 12 August 2020. The empty spaces between the first four 45-foot containers show how the 60-foot IKA wagon platform is less than ideal for this working.

The last section of railway to remain in use on the Trafford Park industrial estate was the Manchester Ship Canal Railway (MSC) branch to Barton Dock Road. Freightliner withdrew from the terminal in 2011, but GBRf introduced a train from Felixstowe to Barton Dock Road later the same year. No. 09002 crosses Park Road on its way from Barton Dock Road to Trafford Park exchange sidings on 20 October 2011. This service lasted only until late 2012 and the MSC branch was then finally abandoned.

After shunning the location for many years, Freightliner returned to Seaforth container terminal in 2021 with trains to Hams Hall and, for a time, Birmingham Lawley Street. No. 66413 *Lest We Forget* shows off its then recently applied Genesee & Wyoming livery as it passes Huyton with 4G99, the 09.03 from Seaforth to Hams Hall, on 21 October 2021.

The unusual pairing of Rail Express Systems-liveried loco No. 86430 *Saint Edmund* and Freightliner classmate No. 86621 *London School of Economics* passes Lowgill on 6 August 2002 with 4S50, the 06.02 from Crewe Basford Hall to Coatbridge. At that time Freightliner ran four trains a day to and from Coatbridge, providing connections with several English ports and terminals.

The year 2006 saw the launch of the high-profile train carrying curtain-sided containers between Daventry and central Scotland, with DRS operating in partnership with haulier Eddie Stobart and retailer Tesco. However, DB took over the business in early 2010. No. 92017 provides appropriate traction for the northbound working, then running as 4S43, the 06.25 from Rugby to Mossend, on 4 January 2010.

The Anglo-Scottish Tesco/Stobart service reverted to DRS in November 2012, initially using a pair of less environmentally friendly Class 66 diesels. However, in October 2013 DRS began hiring a Class 92 electric from DB. No. 92011 *Handel* is in charge of 4S43, the 06.16 from Daventry to Mossend, as it passes Docker on 14 August 2014.

No. 66152 received DB livery in January 2009 and was the only Class 66 in that colour scheme until June 2011. It is pictured passing Oakenshaw Junction shortly after departure with 4L28, the 14.10 Wakefield Europort–Tilbury service, on 18 March 2009. By that time Wakefield Europort had abandoned any idea of handling Channel Tunnel traffic, but was a useful railhead for maritime boxes.

Occupying an 11-acre site alongside the former Midland Railway main line, Leeds Freightliner terminal has stood the test of time since its opening in July 1967. A busy scene is captured on 19 February 2004, as No. 66539 arrives with an incoming train from Felixstowe and No. 66536 waits to depart with 4L85, the 08.58 service to Ipswich.

In 2007 Tees Dock hosted two EWS-hauled intermodal services, one from Mossend and the other from Trafford Park. No. 66231 passes Grangetown just before diverging onto the Tees Dock branch with the incoming Trafford Park train on 1 June 2007. The Mossend business thrived, but the Trafford Park route proved to be unsustainable and the train was later withdrawn.

The TDG railhead at Grangemouth was served initially by Freightliner but later switched to EWS. No. 66096 waits at Grangemouth on 27 August 2003 before departing with 4M67, the 18.01 service to Trafford Park. This train was later amended to start from Mossend, which allowed the mothballing of the Grangemouth terminal. However, the site later returned to use for intermodal trains to and from Tees Dock and Daventry.

Running on electric power, a single Class 88 makes easy work of the gradients on the northern half of the West Coast main line. No. 88005 *Minerva* passes Wandel, between Carstairs and Beattock, with 4M48, the 18.54 Mossend–Daventry service, on 30 June 2021.

Direct Rail Services has continued to run its Mossend–Inverness train on behalf of Tesco, even though its length is restricted to twenty platforms because of the short passing loops on the Highland main line. No. 66422 passes Blackford with 4D47, the 13.10 from Inverness to Mossend, on 2 June 2021. On the right is the nascent Highland Spring railhead, still awaiting its track and container handling equipment.

# Mail and Parcels

The Travelling Post Office (TPO) network included a daily service between Willesden and Dover, which was topped and tailed by Class 73 electro-diesels. Pictured at Kensington Olympia on 23 August 2000 is 1O90, the 16.30 from Willesden to Dover, powered by No. 73131 at the front and No. 73128 at the rear.

EWS ordered its thirty Class 67 diesels primarily with mail traffic in mind. They were kept busy for a few years on non-electrified routes before Royal Mail terminated its contract with the railway prematurely. No. 67003 passes Milford Junction with 1V64, the 14.06 Low Fell–Plymouth train, on 25 August 2000.

Rail Express Systems-liveried loco No. 90016 speeds past South Kenton with 1S96, the 16.00 Willesden–Shieldmuir mail train, on 15 July 2002. Loading to twelve coaches this was one of the longest mail trains on the system. But this was to be the last full year of full-scale Royal Mail operations, as services were wound down during 2003 and finished altogether in early 2004.

Tyne yard was the servicing point for Royal Mail trains to and from Low Fell depot, Newcastle. No. 90032 awaits departure from Tyne yard with 5V28, the 19.02 empty stock working to Low Fell, on 16 July 2003. This will form the overnight TPO service to Bristol. At that time the Royal Mail business was the only regular user of the 25kV catenary in Tyne yard.

Royal Mail's Class 325 electric units were made redundant by the withdrawal of its rail services in early 2004, but made a limited comeback in December of that year when services resumed between Willesden, Warrington and Shieldmuir. Unit No. 325007 leads a twelve-car formation past Rowell between Oxenholme and Carnforth with 1M44, the 15.31 Shieldmuir–Warrington service, on 6 June 2007.

Hopes of a revival of parcels trains were raised in 2021 when Rail Operations Group advertised the launch of its Orion High Speed Logistics Service, using converted Class 319 electric units. A few trial workings took place on the West Coast main line, with the units initially headed by a Class 57 and later running under their own power. No. 57312 hauls units 768001 and 319373 past Daresbury on 15 December 2021 forming 3Q41, the 05.34 from Shieldmuir to Willesden. Unfortunately, by April 2022 there was still no sign of regular services running.

# Wagonload and Niche Markets

EWS used its Enterprise wagonload network to gain a foothold in the intermodal market. No. 66115 heads west on the Great Eastern main line near Chadwell Heath with 6M16, the 09.16 Harwich–Wembley feeder service, on 15 August 2000. The TUA tanks are carrying mud oil from Harwich to Aberdeen, while the flat wagons – mainly FKAs – are loaded with European swapbodies and containers.

One of the last new flows to be attracted to the EWS wagonload network was lime from Dowlow to Fifoots Point power station near Newport. EWS provided a small fleet of refurbished CSA tank wagons for the traffic. The resident Ruston 0-6-0 shunter has just uncoupled from four CSAs at Fifoots Point on 26 October 2000.

Doncaster Belmont yard was reopened in 1998 for cater for wagonload growth to and from Yorkshire and the East Coast ports. Trunk trains connected Belmont with Harwich, Wembley, Bescot, Tees yard, Mossend and Aberdeen. No. 08587 shunts a BYA coil carrier at Belmont on 25 April 2001.

Creative Logistics brought rail freight back to the former Otis distribution terminal at Ordsall Lane, Salford. The company's smartly repainted pilot loco, a Thomas Hill 0-6-0 diesel-hydraulic, No. 01552, shunts IWA vans loaded with tissues from Crailsheim in Germany on 22 May 2001. Unfortunately the Creative Logistics operation did not last long.

The Potter Group terminal at Knowsley gained a rail connection to the Wigan–Kirkby line in 2001, mainly to receive imported paper from Immingham. No. 66093 pauses for the single line token surrender at Rainford with 6E30, the 10.55 Knowsley–Immingham Enterprise service, on 27 July 2001. The containers and most of the vans were returning empty to Immingham, but the five VKA vans in the middle of the train were destined for Inverness.

Lime from Dowlow to Mossend was a wagonload flow that ceased with the demise of Speedlink in 1991 but resumed once the Enterprise network became established. Six lime hoppers form the load for 6F67, the 12.30 trip from Dowlow to Warrington Arpley, on 28 March 2002, with No. 37798 providing the traction. The train has just joined the West Coast main line at Hartford Junction.

The dual voltage Class 92s had regular duties on the West Coast main line in the early 2000s, hauling mainly wagonload and intermodal services. No. 92026 *Britten* passes Headstone Lane with 6X77, the 17.11 Wembley–Mossend Enterprise train, on 20 August 2003. The letter X in the headcode designates a train carrying motor vehicles – in this case Ford cars from Dagenham to Mossend.

No. 47757 *Capability Brown* passes North Stafford Junction with 6G77, the 11.58 Enterprise service from Toton to Bescot, on 17 October 2003. The load includes discharged oil tanks, empty steel carriers, empty scrap wagons and a few intermodal wagons. The intermodal wagons would be detached at Burton-on-Trent. No. 47757 was a former parcels sector locomotive, displaced by the arrival of the Class 67s.

In 2007 the long-standing flow of French bottled water to Neasden was diverted to the recently built Prologis Park distribution centre on the former Coventry Colliery branch. No. 60034 shunts IZA vans at Coventry before departing with 6A51, the 11.40 empties to Wembley, on 29 May 2007. This operation did not last long as the traffic was diverted to Daventry in November 2009.

One of the last cross-Channel wagonload flows was chlorofluoromethane from north-west England to Germany, loaded in ICA/ICB tank wagons. No. 67028 approaches Arpley Junction with train 6F44, the 10.10 from Ditton to Arpley, on 12 February 2008. The loading point for this traffic was later switched from Ditton to Warrington Dallam.

No. 60040 was named *The Territorial Army Centenary* at the National Railway Museum in June 2008. At the same time it received a unique livery of all-over EWS maroon, but without any EWS branding. It is pictured passing Chester with 6F80, the 14.50 Holyhead–Warrington Arpley Enterprise trip, on 25 April 2009, conveying vans from Anglesey Aluminium. The maroon livery gave way to standard DB red in 2012.

No. 37401 was the only active Class 37 on EWS's books when the company was rebranded DB Schenker in January 2009. It is seen near the site of Bold colliery hauling 6F14, the 08.32 Liverpool Docks–Warrington Arpley wagonload trip, on 1 May 2009. The train is conveying five empty IWB/IWA vans returning from Stanton Grove to Immingham for reloading with imported paper.

EWS and its successor DB served the MoD's Central Vehicle Depot at Ashchurch by an 'as required' train from Didcot. No. 67002 arrives in the loop at Ashchurch with Warflat and Warwell wagons forming 7X36, the 04.55 departure from Didcot, on 1 September 2010. The train had run round at Worcester in order to approach Ashchurch from the north and set back onto the MoD branch.

The 2-mile branch to Donnington reopened in February 2009 to serve the grandly named Telford International Railfreight Park. Traffic was sparse from the outset, with just occasional deliveries of containers for the nearby MoD depot. On hire from DRS to DB, No. 37610 has just set back into the unloading area at Donnington with 6G51, the 07.51 feeder service from Warrington Arpley, on 25 August 2011.

Eastleigh was the base for MoD trips to Marchwood and the interface with what remained of DB's wagonload network. No. 66085 has just pulled out of Eastleigh yard with 6B45, the 09.14 trip to Marchwood, on 2 March 2017. At that time it was rare to see such a healthy load on the Marchwood trip.

GB Railfreight took over the MoD contract in 2017 and replaced the DB wagonload trips with direct services running as required between terminals. Trains to Donnington could originate as far afield as Bicester, Kineton or Carlisle and were usually routed via Crewe to avoid a reversal at Wellington or Shrewsbury. No.66751 *Inspirational Delivered Hitachi Rail Europe* passes Wrenbury with sixteen VKA/VGA vans forming 6G84, the 07.24 Kineton–Donnington service, on 17 January 2022.

The Kronospan chipboard factory at Chirk regained its rail service in 1997 as EWS developed its Enterprise network. No. 66096 waits while its train of MBA wagons is unloaded at the Kronospan terminal on 15 January 2000. By this time most of the timber came from Carlisle and the West Highlands and EWS operated a direct train from Carlisle to Chirk, calling at Warrington Arpley for additional traffic.

Timber to Chirk was one of the first EWS wagonload flows to switch to a competing freight company. The traffic was taken over by AMEC-SPIE in December 2006 and became a Colas Rail operation when AMEC-SPIE and SECO Rail merged to form Colas Rail in July 2007. For traction, a hired Virgin Class 57/3 was used. No. 57313 *Tracy Island* passes Rossett with 6J37, the 13.27 from Carlisle, on 9 August 2007.

Colas Rail adopted Carlisle yard as one of its main timber-loading points, handling logs from the Kielder Forest. No. 66850 shunts KFA wagons at Carlisle ready to form 6J37, the 12.50 departure to Chirk, on 19 July 2011. This locomotive began its life as Freightliner No. 66557 and was transferred to Colas Rail in June 2011.

Alongside the well-established flow from Carlisle, Kronospan sourced some of its timber from south-west England. No. 70804 passes Parson Street on the outskirts of Bristol with 6V54, the 05.35 Chirk–Exeter Riverside empties, on 15 April 2015. The first three wagons are former high cube KSAs, which had recently been converted for timber traffic.

Colas Rail made regular use of its Class 56 locomotives on timber trains from Baglan Bay to Chirk, routed via the Marches line. No. 56094 passes Ponthir with 6Z51, the 16.02 departure from Baglan Bay, on 16 June 2021. This locomotive was one of the first four Class 56s that Colas Rail acquired in 2012.